DID YOU KNOW . . .

- that kittens, like children, lose their baby teeth, or milk teeth, before an adult set of thirty teeth appears?
- that the old saying "a cat always lands on its feet" is not true?
- that when a cat means business in a fight, it lies on its back and attacks with its claws, thus protecting its spine?
- that the cat has the most sensitive sense of touch of all mammals?

This book contains the answers to all of your questions about raising a happy, healthy cat, plus many unusual and interesting facts.

Cinnamon (cindy) Chubbs

Tiger Bloch

Samantha (Sam) J. Pusskins

Lady Guinevere (Gwenie)

Max

Marcus Garvey and Rudi

Jasmina Hamdan

Cat Femenella

Marmalade, domestic shorthair, age three
months. Marmalade lives in the rather heady
atmosphere of the Massachusetts Institute of
Technology campus, but once in a while he
just likes to get away from it all and
climb a tree.

CATS & KITTENS

by Jane Rockwell

AN ARCHWAY PAPERBACK
POCKET BOOKS • NEW YORK

POCKET BOOKS, a Simon & Schuster division of
GULF & WESTERN CORPORATION
1230 Avenue of the Americas, New York, N.Y. 10020

ISBN: 0-671-56039-5

First Pocket Books printing December, 1979

10 9 8 7 6 5 4 3 2 1

Trademarks registered in the United States and other countries.

Printed in the U.S.A.

Acknowledgments

The author and publishers wish to thank the following for their permission to use the material listed below:

The Atlantic Monthly, for "I Am the Cat" by Guy Bogart. Material appears on page xiii.

Alfred A. Knopf, Inc., for excerpt from "The Abandoned" by Paul Gallico, copyright 1950. Material appears on page 95.

Material on page 41 is from "Cats and Their Care" by Henrietta Hitchcock. *New York World-Telegram and Sun;* © 1952 by the New York World-Telegram Corporation.

PHOTO CREDITS

Photo research by Selma Hamdan
Diagrams by Vantage Art, Inc.

Photographs courtesy of: ASPCA—pp. 64; British Museum—pp. 4; Charles Phelps Cushing—pps. xii (by Ward Alan Howe), 16, 21, 24, 36, 40, 46 (by John Sybenga); Nancy Lehrer—pp. 89; Miston Cattery—pp. 91; Monkmeyer Press Photo Service—pp. 83; Mrs. Richard Negus—pp. 78; Janet J. Peters—pp. 85; David Bruce Rawcliffe—pp. 62; Ima N. Roe—pp. 88; Sun Dance Abyssinians—pp. 80; UPI—pps. vi, xviii, 9, 27, 28, 31, 52, 57, 70, 82; Wide World—pps. 79, 80, 86.

TO MAX AND BLOSSOM,
*my faithful feline companions
for many, many years—*

AND TO KAVI, AND E. B.,
my new-found friends.

I AM THE CAT
by Guy Bogart

I am the Cat—
   Serve me,
   Love me
   Play with me,
   Enjoy me,
   Live with me,
   And I repay.

I am the Cat—
   With claws and fangs when I must!
   With purrs and caresses when I may!
   Tiger and Cherub
   I walk with folks,
   Yet only on terms of equality.
   Subservient to none
   I am the companion to man.
   I am Love and Beauty
   Fidelity and Felicity
I am the Cat.

Contents

CATS & KITTENS

Cats display unusual grace and agility, even when they are very young. These kittens are playing with a twig.

Characteristics of the Cat

Cats are exceptional members of the animal kingdom.

Their relatives are lions and tigers and other wild animals that inhabit the jungles and forests. But this book is about the familiar domestic cat, or *Felis catus* as it is called by zoologists.

Felis catus is among the most intelligent of animals. A cat's brain roughly resembles that of a human being, and laboratory tests have shown that a cat's intelligence is higher than that of dogs, raccoons, and rats. Of course, this isn't true of all cats. Like man, among cats there is a wide range in degrees of intelligence and ability.

Cats are distinguished also for their extreme independence. Unlike dogs, they go their own way and make up their own minds about what they will—or won't!—do.

Blossom, a tabby cat I once had, is an ideal example. If Blossom didn't want to sit on my lap, no amount of coaxing would make her do so. On the other hand, if Blossom did want to sit with me, she'd jump on my lap and curl up on the newspaper or magazine I was trying to read.

Authorities agree that it is nearly impossible to force a cat to do anything it doesn't want to do. But if you try to understand and accept your cat's independent ways, you will find it to be loving and affectionate toward you.

No other animal is as graceful and agile as a cat. If you have ever seen a cat stalking a bird or leaping into the air to catch a butterfly, you have noticed that its body moves with smooth, near-perfect precision. It is a joy to watch, even if you are worried that it may, indeed, catch that chattering blue jay or that lovely butterfly.

A Long and Colorful History

No one really knows how and when the domestic cat first appeared on earth, although there are many theories. However, there is reason to believe that cats were domesticated by man about 5,000 years ago. The first written reference to cats occurred in Egypt where the cat goddess, Bastet (or Pasht), was worshiped. Bastet was seen as a human figure on a totem pole with the head of a cat.

Cat worship by the Egyptians went on for centuries, and cat figurines adorned with jewelry and other finery have been found in Egypt's tombs.

In fact, cats were so revered that the penalty was heavy for Egyptians who were caught killing them. When a cat died, it wasn't unusual for human members of a household to cut off their eyebrows to show their grief.

Cats, like many human beings of that time, were mummified. And even more

The cat goddess Bastet was worshipped in Egypt centuries ago.

amazing, archeologists have found mummified mice buried along with the cats to provide food in the afterlife. In those days a human funeral cost the equivalent of $1,500; a cat funeral amounted to about $500!

Cats also were worshiped in other countries. In China during the Hsia, Shang, and Chou dynasties (from 2205 to 225 B.C.), sacrificial rites and theatrical ceremonies were held in their honor and, like the Egyptians, a stiff penalty was imposed for their destruction.

Since the beginning of time, cats have played a significant role in the history of man. Cat clans in the Teutonic and Celtic countries proudly used the animals as emblems for their banners. Roman soldiers displayed cat figures on their shields, as did soldiers of other nationalities, including the Norsemen, forerunners of the Scandinavian people. The Norse goddess Freya is often shown in a chariot drawn by two cats. Norse maidens were married on Freya's day (Friday) if at all possible. If the sun shone during the ceremony, it was said that the maiden had taken good care of the cat and fed it well.

Cats spread throughout the world when

soldiers and sailors adopted them as mascots to serve as rat-killers aboard ship. How important they were to the seagoing world is shown by such terms as *catwalk*, meaning a high, narrow passageway; *cathead*, where the ship's anchor was hoisted; and *cat-o'-nine-tails*, a whip with which sailors were flogged.

Superstitions and Myths

It hasn't always been a "bed of catnip" for our feline friends, however. During witchcraft days in Europe and America, cats were considered companions to witches and, as such, omens of bad luck. In the early 1700's, people still believed that witches sometimes took the shape of cats and that witches and cats spoke the same language. Many persons still think that a black cat is an omen of bad luck—especially when it crosses one's path. (More than once I've watched a houseguest shudder when my black cat, Max, came unexpectedly into the living room!)

In ancient Egypt and Japan, spiritualists believed that cats protected people from supernatural forces. Many Orientals credited the cat with the ability to see in the past and forecast the future and also to see beings and objects invisible to man. Even today, the feline habit of looking steadily and unblinkingly at someone, or of sitting for long periods with half-closed eyes, gives the cat the reputation for being "all knowing" and wise.

In the seventeenth century, cats were considered excellent weather predictors. A cat washing its face toward the wind, or an elderly cat frisking about, meant that a storm was brewing. When a cat sat with its back to the fire, it was thought that a frost was coming.

These ideas aren't as far-fetched as they sound. Scientists have reported that cats' supersensitive hearing powers have enabled them to pick up the ground vibrations that precede a hurricane.

However, superstitions and myths through the ages have led to many false ideas about cats. The common belief that cats see in total darkness simply isn't so. But it is a fact that a cat's eyes are constructed so its night vision is superior to that of a human being.

Contrary to popular belief, cats are often hurt or killed in falls from high places, and once up a tree they may not be able to get down alone.

The old saying that a cat has nine lives is now treated lightly, but many people still think that a cat can fall many stories and emerge alive, and even unhurt. Again, not so. Feline grace and sinewy muscles may spare a cat harm in a short tumble, but many cats die every year in falls from high places. If you have seen (or heard) a cat that has been "treed" by a dog or one that has climbed too high in a tree, you know that usually it is frightened and is asking to be rescued. Years ago, my cat Sidney was chased by a dog and climbed nearly to the top of a giant oak tree. It took an outstretched blanket held by three friends and me and a great deal of coaxing to convince him that landing on the blanket was his only salvation. All of us, including Sidney, were very relieved when he landed unhurt in the middle of the blanket.

Anatomy and Physiology

The cat is a mammal (an animal that feeds its young with milk from the mammary glands), as is man, and it belongs to the order *Carnivora* (flesh-eating mammals), as do dogs, among others. The cat's body is made up of over 250 bones, some 517 muscles, and a slight amount of fat. Its construction gives the body great elasticity. In man, the spinal column is held together by ligaments, but in the cat it is connected by muscles, which make it very flexible. A cat can elongate or contract its back, can curve it upward in an arc, and can even make it quiver from side to side. The mobility of the spinal column is greatest in the tail, which can be bent in any direction. The construction of the cat's shoulder joint allows it to turn its forelegs in many directions. The very small and sometimes nonexistent clavicle (collarbone) also permits much freedom of movement.

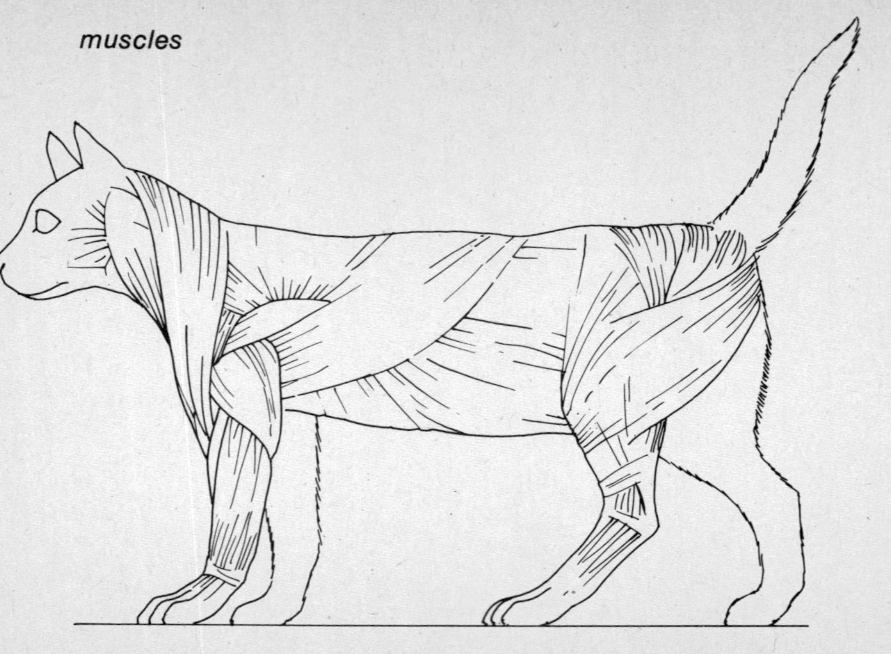
muscles

Unlike man, the cat has no thumb, but it does have what is almost a thumb attached to the inside of the top of its forefoot. A bone never developed there—only the claw remains as a hint of what might have been if the cat's evolutionary pattern had been different. What the cat lacks in thumbs, it makes up in toes. Most cats have five toes on their forefeet (including the "thumb") and four toes on their hind feet. But they can have as many as seven toes on one foot. This is an inherited trait and can occur in all breeds.

Cats walk on their toes, not on the soles of their feet. When they walk and run, they move the front and back legs on one side and then the front and back legs on the other side. Other four-footed animals that move this way naturally are the camel and the giraffe. When cats walk, their natural slippers—their pads—protect and insulate their feet.

The claws, natural weapons of the cat, are sharp, curved, and adapted to grasping. Normally they are hidden, but they quickly come into view when needed! Since a cat's claws can be drawn in or extended, they are said to be retractile. (A bear's claws, for instance, are not retractile—they are always out.)

A cat's teeth come in two installments—milk teeth and adult teeth. At about six months, the milk teeth are shed and what will be a total of thirty adult teeth appear. This set of teeth is usually complete by about eight months.

The tongue of the cat is long and flat and contains a muscular fiber known as the *lytta*. This accounts for the lapping action you see and hear when the cat drinks liquids. The tongue also has tiny, sharp bumps, or *papillae*, that allow it to scrape meat off bones and to lick its furry coat clean. The cat's tongue can reach every part of its body except the center of its back and neck. So if you want to hear your cat purr happily, just scratch it between its shoulder blades. Maybe it will thank you by licking your hand with its tongue, which it also uses to show affection.

The coat holds a layer of air close to the skin that helps insulate the cat's body against changes in temperature. An undercoat of fine hair is overlaid by longer and coarser hair. Attached to the hair follicles are tiny muscles that cause the hair to stand up when the cat is angry or fright-

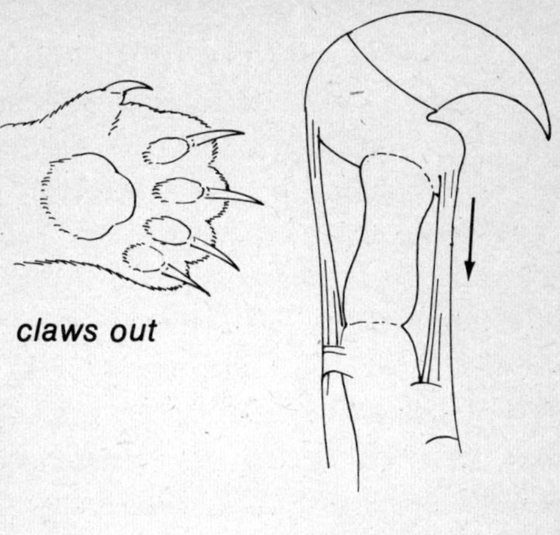

claws out

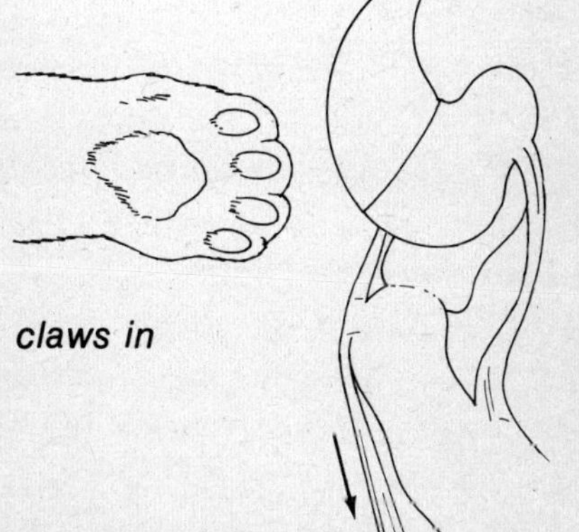

claws in

ened. This is used as a defense to frighten enemies. In spring and autumn the coat is noticeably shed and regrown, although some shedding goes on all the time.

The cat's eyebrows and whiskers *(vibrissae)* are coarse and wiry. They protect the eyes and act as feelers. The bulbs of these hairs are rich in nerve and blood supply and make the hairs very sensitive. Many people think the purpose of whiskers is to test passageways to determine if they are wide enough for the cat's body to pass through. This is not true. How many cats have you seen whose whiskers are as wide or wider than their bodies? However, the whiskers do help the cat to feel its way along when it cannot see.

Although many thousands of unwanted cats die every year from neglect or malnutrition, new drugs and improved veterinary practices have helped to increase the average lifetime of our feline friends. Over the past few years a cat's life expectancy has increased from twelve to seventeen years, and some have lived thirty years.

The
Senses

HEARING

Cats respond much as man does to low frequencies, but they are much more sensitive than man is to high frequencies of sound. A cat reacts to tones of up to 60,000 cycles per second. The ear of the cat contains more than thirty muscles (man has six) that enable it to collect sound waves from several directions. Semicircular canals in the inner ear give the cat its excellent sense of balance and help it to land on its feet after a fall.

SMELL

Cats have a delicate sense of smell. They are partial to the fragrance of flowers, some colognes, mint, some vegetables, and, of course, catnip. They also appreciate other odors such as the gas and oil used in cars,

In strong light a cat's pupils shrink to slits.

freshly slaughtered meat, plaster, and stagnant water from flower vases. Unlike dogs, however, they are not attracted to the powerful odors of carrion (rotting meat) or excrement.

SIGHT

As we know, cats can see much better in the dark than man can and better than most animals in faint light. The surface of a cat's eye is very large in proportion to its body and the pupils are very sensitive. In strong light a cat's pupils shrink to slits; in poor light they expand until they cover nearly the entire surface of the eye. Normally, age does not dim their visual powers. Cats have an unusual ability to adjust the focus of their eyes to distance. Have you seen a cat jump several feet into the air and make a neat landing on a spot about half as big as it is? Cats can distinguish shapes better than dogs, but not as well as man. They can tell the difference between squares and circles, but not designs on those squares and circles. Most cat researchers agree that cats cannot distinguish shades of color.

TASTE

Long, pointed canine teeth and sharp-edged molars enable a cat to tear its food, crush it up, and swallow it quickly. Therefore, food does not stay in their mouths very long. Because of this, cats are thought not to have much of a sense of taste and to rely mainly on their sense of smell.

TOUCH

Authorities generally agree that the cat has the most sensitive sense of touch of all mammals. Every hair on its coat is sensitive, particularly those on its front paws. (I never fail to be amazed when one of my cats walks along the crowded mantel above my fireplace without disturbing one single object on it.)

ELECTRICITY AND TEMPERATURE

You may have noticed that a cat "generates" its own electricity when you stroke the hair on its back. One engineer discovered that the electric potential on a

An angry cat displays the long canine teeth and sharp-edged molars that allow it to tear and crush food and swallow it quickly.

cat's back was enough to light a 75-watt light bulb!

Anything that gives off heat attracts cats. As soon as the summer sun is gone, they go in search of a radiator or fireplace. They can sit for hours in front of that radiator or fireplace and suddenly pick themselves up and head for an outing in the snow. Why? Their bodies are equipped to adapt easily to extremes in temperature.

Animal psychologists have defined the environment of the cat as being made up of three elements: vital domain, territory, and lair. The *vital domain,* also called home ground, is the place where the cat lives, hunts, and plays. The *territory* is located inside the vital domain. It is the cozy armchair, the top of the refrigerator, or the footstool by the fireplace—areas that the cat will defend against other cats or invaders. The *lair* is the precise spot within the vital domain where the cat takes refuge to rest, to escape from danger, or just to be alone.

Cats are loners. They do not run in packs as dogs often do. Curiously enough, if they are forced to live in groups, they adapt more readily than dogs. In that situation, there is a definite power system. One cat is in charge. It does not have to be the strongest, or the oldest, or a male, but simply the cat that can dominate all the

*This cat's territory seems
to be the front of the fireplace.*

others. If a new cat enters the domain, usually there is a battle for dominance. The "top cat" arches its back, spits, thrashes its tail back and forth, and bares its claws. Next, there is a fight, or, if the challenger decides to adopt an attitude of submission (flattening itself on the ground), the dominant cat seizes the other by the scruff of the neck and straddles it for a few seconds to show officially who is boss!

HUNTING AND FIGHTING

Many people are shocked when they see cats killing birds, squirrels, and other wildlife. But people lead lambs and calves to slaughter and enjoy eating lobsters that have been boiled alive. They teach dogs to hunt, but object to cats hunting on their own. We must remember that cats are carnivorous, or meat-eaters—more so than man. They are only obeying their instincts when they prey upon other animals. My cat Kavi at times will deposit a mouse at my feet and look up expectantly for praise. As difficult as it may be, I have learned to thank him, not scold him.

Unless it is cornered, a cat seldom will

Left, although these part-Maltese kittens do not seem very fierce even in battle, it is best to stay away from fighting cats. Above, tail straight up indicates pride and contentment; no wonder, this cat, who lives on a farm in Wisconsin, has its own private street crossing.

fight with a dog. When a cat must fight, it jumps on the dog's back and clings there while tearing at the dog's head and eyes with its claws. (Ironically, the cat's worst enemy, the eagle, can do the same thing to the cat.) In a cat-dog fight, the cat usually is the winner.

When a cat really means business in a fight, it lies on its back and brings its claws into play, thus protecting its spine, which is its most vulnerably spot. Usually the most damage it suffers is a torn ear or scarred tail. If a cat cries during a fight, it is usually a battle cry, not a cry for help.

Never touch a fighting cat. In the excitement, the cat could turn on you and claw you badly, not meaning to. If the fight is a serious one, use a pail of water or make the loudest noise possible to break it up. And stay a good ten feet away from the problem!

LANGUAGE

The language of cats is a study in itself. It is made up of various mews, hisses, screams, growls, spits, and caterwauls, which we'll speak of later.

Everyone knows that a contented cat purrs, but how many people know that a cat also purrs when it is in extreme pain? A purr that is caused by extreme pain is a harsher, deeper sound than is the pleasure purr.

Cats have an impressive vocabulary. The familiar *meow* is used only in conversations with humans, not with other cats. The *chirrup* is used both as a greeting and a comment with man and with other animals. When I opened a door for my cat Max (who could not stand to see a door closed), his *chirrup* meant "Thank you," or in some cases, "It's about time!" If I came into a room unexpectedly, his surprised *chirrup* meant, "Oh, hi!"

A cat's tail is a good barometer of its feelings. In general, we can say that when the tail is raised straight up it means the cat is contented and proud. If it is straight out, it is stalking or frightened. If it is curled under its body, it is scared or worried. When it twitches, it is amused or pleased. When it is thrashing from side to side, it is annoyed or angry.

Cats are considered among the most, if not *the* most, sexual of all the members of the animal kingdom. They are quite unorthodox where sex is concerned. For instance, sexual excitement can lead a tom to try to straddle either a male or female or even a completely different species of animal. A female in heat goes in search of a male, but if a male is not available, she may rub up against a person, purring noisily and giving little affectionate knocks with her head.

A female in heat grovels on her stomach, rolls on her back, or twists her body around and around. Some lower their heads and paw the ground. If someone pets her, she may hollow her back and present herself in the mating position.

Cats are very vocal at mating time. The female's cries almost always accompany the act. The "song" that males and females sing at this time is called *caterwauling*. Researchers are certain that caterwauling is associated with sexual activity, because neutered cats never caterwaul. I am sure you have been awakened more than once by caterwauling cats. If two toms are involved, their duet usually ends in a duel in which one knocks the other from the fence or wall where the concert took place.

In the case of cats that do not live under the same roof or cats living in the wild, mating can last for several days or until the male (or males) is exhausted. And that brings up a phenomenon of cat reproduction—dual mating. When cats are allowed to mate at will, it is probable that a female, or queen as she is called, will have a litter that has been fathered by several males. The female produces several eggs in a litter. One egg can be fertilized by one tom, another by a second tom, and so on, depending upon how many toms have mated with the female and how many eggs there are.

NEUTERING

Most authorities agree that if you are not going to breed and show your cat, you are

*These three kittens from the same litter
may each have a different father.*

doing everyone a favor, including your cat, if you have it neutered. Usually, your cat is a better and happier pet when this is done. Freed from its powerful sex drive, other facets of the cat's personality come out. Also, you won't have to patch torn ears and other battle scars that accompany a cat's sex life. Neither will you have to put up with the offensive odor produced by the unaltered male when he sprays, or urinates, and the unruly and often destructive behavior of the female when she is in heat. Spaying, removing the ovaries (reproductive glands) and altering, or castrating, should take place early—from four or six months—when they are relatively simple operations. But you should consult your veterinarian. That is the wisest way to determine what is best for the individual cat.

Spaying the female requires an incision in the abdomen, an anesthetic, and a few days' hospitalization to insure that the cat heals properly. Altering the male is a simpler operation, but it does require an anesthetic since the testes, or reproductive glands, are removed.

It is often said that neutered cats become fat and lazy, but this need not happen. If a cat gets enough exercise and is not over-fed, its physical appearance after neutering will be unchanged, except perhaps for a slightly thicker coat of hair.

Maternal Behavior

Most female cats have a well-developed maternal instinct. Before giving birth, the female searches carefully for a proper nest. You can help her by selecting a large cardboard box, which has a door cut out on one side high enough (about eight inches) so that the kittens can't get out. Line the box with torn, shredded newspapers so that the mother-to-be can push them around to her heart's content. When she has arranged the box the way she wants it, lay a blanket over the paper and a towel on top, which you can remove and wash.

A female is ready to become pregnant after about six months of age. The pregnancy can run from fifty-seven to sixty-nine days, with the average sixty-two days. A month after mating, you will know she is pregnant if you can feel small lumps in her abdomen. These are the developing fetuses. After you have determined that the

offspring are on the way, do not coddle the future mother.

Your cat's diet should remain unchanged until the last two or three weeks when it is all right to give her an additional meal. Beware of overfeeding—a fat cat may have difficulty giving birth. You can add a little calcium to her diet, but it is not necessary to give her additional milk. A pregnant cat can run and jump as usual until two or three days before the births occur.

THE BIRTH PROCESS

The normal cat gives birth with little effort or discomfort. The average litter consists of three to four kittens, and the process takes about two to three hours, although the time may vary according to the cat.

Each kitten arrives completely enclosed in a semitransparent membrane or sac. When the kitten is born it is attached to the umbilical cord, which is attached to the placenta, or afterbirth. The mother tears open the sac around the kitten, nips the umbilical cord with her teeth, and eats the placenta. Then she cleans the kitten thor-

A mother cat nurses her furry, growing kittens.

oughly from head to toe. Don't be alarmed if she seems rough with the baby kitten. She is just stimulating its breathing and circulation systems.

If a newborn kitten doesn't start to breathe before the next one begins to arrive, you had better lend a hand. Gently swing the kitten by its back legs until it gasps for breath.

If the mother has not cut the umbilical cord close enough (about one-half inch from its body) cut the longer portion with a dull pair of scissors and apply a drop of iodine to the end of the cord.

If for some reason the mother cannot or will not take care of her kittens after the births, you can help by removing any membrane material and cleaning the nostrils to prevent danger of suffocation.

Most cats do not want assitance when giving birth, but if no kitten appears one hour after labor starts, you can help. If you feel the tail and hind legs of the unborn kitten, take hold with a piece of cloth and pull gently, but firmly. No tugging. The mother will probably strain to help you. If you do not feel capable of doing this—and it is probably advisable only in dire circumstances—call a veterinary surgeon. *Remember, do not interfere unless you feel it is absolutely necessary.*

DOS AND DON'TS AFTER BIRTH

- *Don't* try to persuade the mother to eat for twenty-four hours after the big event if she doesn't want to. *Do* put water near the box and a bowl of milk if you think she needs nourishment.
- *Don't* interfere with the new family and *don't* bring an army of visitors to see them. *Do* baby-sit with the kittens if the mother indicates she would like "to get away from it all" for awhile.
- *Don't* expose the kittens' eyes to strong light for a full month. Their eyes should open, however, after about twelve days.

CHOWDER
TO TAKE OUT
CHOICE CATS
SOLD BY THE POUND

Choosing Your Kitten

Don't go in for cats if you must have obedience in a pet. They are the most independent, defiant little souls in the animal world. You must love them for their funniness, their gentle affection, their perfect understanding of your moods, their pathetic dependence on your love even while they are teasing you. (Excerpt from Cats and Their Care *by Henrietta Hitchcock, copyright 1952 by the New York World Telegram Corporation.*)

If you want a kitten but do not have one born into your household, you will have to go in search of one. There are several possibilities.

Unfortunately for cats, but fortunately for you, there are many more cats than there are homes for them. Recent estimates put the cat population in the United States at more than 40 million.

The classified section of your local

newspaper usually contains ads stating something like, "Four darling kittens free to good homes." But if you have a definite idea of the kitten you want, you will have to pay for your pet, and if you want a pedigreed cat you will have to buy it from a breeder, a cat show, or a pet shop.

Whatever your source, here are a few points to keep in mind when deciding on your feline companion for years to come.

- Never buy a kitten from a place that smells of cat odors. Obviously the sanitary conditions are not the best, and it would be wise to go elsewhere.
- Do not buy a kitten that is less than six weeks old. Even better, wait until it is eight or nine weeks. If an examination reveals a full set of sharp, white teeth and a clear, rosy pink mouth inside, the kitten is a good candidate.
- Never buy a kitten that runs but does not walk. A kitten that runs and falls, runs a few more steps and falls again may look awfully cute, but it is a risky bet since it is more difficult for a kitten to walk than run and even more difficult to walk slowly. Its sense of balance or coordination may be faulty.

- Look at the entire litter, not only the one you have singled out. You soon will see that there is a leader—one more aggressive than the others. If you want a cat that is very affectionate, think twice about choosing the leader.
- Pull a piece of string across the floor and watch how the individual kittens react. No normal kitten can resist a piece of string wiggling in front of it. In all probability you'll discover which kitten is quickest and which one is the most clever.
- When you have decided on the kitten you want, examine it carefully. Let it examine you, too. Put your hand, palm up, on the floor and wiggle your fingers until the kitten comes and sniffs it. If the kitten backs up, bushes its tail, and spits, think twice. Chances are it's nervous, and nervous kittens become nervous cats. If it comes to your hand willingly, stroke its head gently with one finger of your other hand. After it begins to purr, pick up the kitten and place it against your shoulder with its head touching your cheek. Continue to stroke it, talking to it softly. Soon its purr will become

regular and it will cuddle against you with complete trust.

- When the kitten trusts you is the ideal time to examine its body. First, the ears. Do not poke inside them, but take a good look and a good sniff. If there is any odor, do not buy the kitten. A kitten of that age should have no ear problems. If it has, it has been badly neglected. Run your hand gently over the body. It should be soft and smooth. If you feel any roughness, part the hairs and have a close look. It may be only a scratch, but if it looks like a sore, be careful. It could be the beginning of something contagious and simply not worth the risk. The kitten's stomach should feel firm and rubbery with the same sort of give as a rubber ball. If it is soft and flabby, something is wrong.

All of this might lead you to think that it is difficult to find a healthy kitten. Not so. Chances are extremely good that you will find a perfectly sound kitten in reputable pet stores and private homes.

Here's another important point to remember: It is advisable to know how to tell the sex of the kitten. Mistakes are made often. During the first twenty-four

male

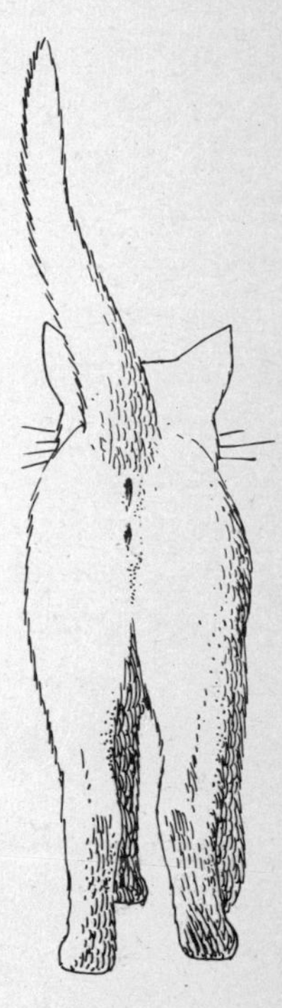

female

Kittens are full of energy and curiosity, and they love to explore a new home.

hours after birth, it is easy to distinguish males and females. But afterward there is a period when it is very difficult to tell. Keep in mind that the sex organs of the male appear as a soft bunch and those of the female appear flat. If you look closely at the female you will see a tiny slit in the genital area.

When you have your new kitten at home, make it feel welcome and comfortable. The first few weeks, and particularly the first few days, are crucial. Suddenly the kitten is without its mother and brothers and sisters in entirely new surroundings. Since you will need time to make the new member of the family feel at home, it is best not to bring the kitten into your household at a busy time. At the very least, devote the first two days to your new arrival. Usually the weekend is the best time for the kitten's introduction to its new home.

At first, activity should be kept to a minimum around the kitten. But it should be allowed to follow its instinct to explore every nook and cranny of the new—and strange—place.

Aside from a drink of milk on arrival, don't try to feed the kitten until it has gotten the wanderlust out of its system. When your friend begins to feel at home, it will probably sit down and wash itself. That is the time to offer the kitten its first meal.

Be affectionate with your new kitten. Hold it on your lap and against your shoulder, stroke it, and talk to it quietly. Conversation, to my way of thinking, is extremely important. I have always talked to my cats from the beginning of our friendships. Soon they begin to understand me and soon they begin talking to me, too.

Kittens are full of energy and need to play hard, but they also need a lot of sleep. They go from playing to sleeping as quickly as you can blink an eye. Although a kitten requires much attention, don't give it when it isn't wanted. If the kitten wants to jump down from your lap, let it. If you try to hold it against its will, you will undo the effect of much of the warmth and affection you have given it.

Caring for Your Kitten

A new kitten in your home, whether it came from a cat breeder or from a neighbor, needs certain things done for it. First, and most important, is a visit to the veterinarian. There it will be checked for worms, enteritis (distemper), rabies, and pneumonitis, a highly contagious disease caused by several viruses. After the first visit, you will be returning from time to time for checkups and booster shots as your vet advises.

PARASITES—INTERNAL AND EXTERNAL

There are a number of diseases and illnesses to which kittens are susceptible. One of the most common is parasites.

Internal parasites, or those that can live inside the kitten's body, are hookworms, tapeworms, roundworms, and whipworms. By studying the kitten's stool under a microscope, your vet will be able to tell if worms are present and what kind they are. Fortunately, the treatment is simple, and the recovery rapid.

Fleas, lice, ticks, and earmites are external parasites that can live on the body. Fleas are far more common than lice on kittens and cats. Fleas are carriers of disease and can spread tapeworms. There are many effective powders and sprays on the market for both fleas and lice. Under no condition, however, should you use a preparation containing DDT, a chemical that has been shown to be harmful to man and other animals. Apply powders or sprays to the kitten's sleeping areas as well as to the kitten itself.

Ticks are eight-legged creatures resembling spiders. They imbed themselves in the skin of an animal and fill their bodies with the animal's blood. To remove a tick, put alcohol or vinegar on it and pull it out with a pair of tweezers. Be sure to remove the whole tick. Infections can develop around the place where the tick has entered the skin. If you find many ticks, have your veterinarian use a preparation especially made for cats.

If a kitten constantly shakes its head and scratches its ears, it probably has earmites. Mites cause scabs and make the kitten's ears look and smell dirty. An unusual accumulation of dirt and wax is a breeding ground for mites, so it is important to take your kitten to the vet immediately if you suspect earmites.

As a rule, cats cannot transmit diseases to man, but recently, medical science discovered an exception—a parasitic infection called *toxoplasmosis*. This infection generally is a mild one to humans and after one infection, they are immune. But if the disease is caught by a pregnant woman, it can result in birth defects to her unborn child. If the digestive system of a cat becomes infected with the parasite, another infective stage called *oocysts* will be excreted in the feces of the animal. After a short period of time—two to four days—these oocysts become infective to other animals and to man.

Cats can be reinfected by eating raw meat, mice, or other animals or by contact with other infected cats. The veterinarian

Hopefully, this group is healthy! All these cats belong to this farm lady in Wisconsin, because, she says, she just likes cats.

can determine if your cat is infected by testing a sample of its feces. Toxoplasmosis is a good reason to make sure your cat's box is cleaned daily.

SKIN DISEASES

Mange, ringworm, and eczema are three diseases of the skin to watch out for. There are two types of mange. One shows excessive shedding of hair and bald spots around the eyes. The other is harder to recognize because it results only in a reddening of the eyes. Get your cat to the vet immediately if you suspect it has mange. Treatment is effective only if the disease is diagnosed early.

Bare patches on the skin starting around the head signify ringworm, a very contagious condition. You can treat it with iodine, but if it continues to spread, see your veterinarian.

Eczema can be identified by intense itching, particularly along the cat's back and around the base of its tail. Shedding of hair and scaly skin usually accompany the itching. Eczema can be caused by an imbalance of hormones or an allergy of the kitten to its diet or environment. Your veterinarian will prescribe a proper treatment.

OTHER AILMENTS

Tooth and gum trouble can be caused by tartar—hard, calciumlike deposits—like that which forms in the human mouth. Just as the dentist does, your veterinarian will remove these deposits if they occur.

Gingivitis, another condition shared by man, usually is marked by bright redness around the base of the teeth and by sensitive gums. If this condition is left untreated, it can result in loss of teeth.

Another ailment to which cats are subject is constipation, which can be caused by hairballs in the stomach or by improper diet. Older cats are more apt to have this problem, but daily grooming and a teaspoon of salad oil or butter and a meal of raw liver will help both kitten and adult cat to conquer this condition. Commercial medicine, in salve or paste form, also can be used. Apply them to the kitten's lips or forepaws to insure that they are swallowed immediately.

Vomiting and diarrhea are symptoms of illness. Limit your kitten's diet to small amounts of liquid. If either condition continues, or if it is bloody, see your vet.

Do not be too concerned about the least little sneeze or scratch. A sneeze may not be a cold; it may be just a speck of dust in the nostrils. A scratch may not be a flea, but just a tickle. Speaking of scratching, you will soon be able to tell if your kitten is scratching because it means business or because there isn't anything better to do at the moment.

HOME CARE

There could be a time when your kitten is sick, but not sick enough to be taken to the animal hospital. Or there could be a time when it is recuperating at home after an illness or accident. If this occurs, here are a few hints on caring for your animal at home.

A sick or injured kitten may not be able to wash itself. In that case, use a damp washcloth and a mild soap.

Keep your kitten in a quiet area of the house where it won't be disturbed, and where it will be free of dampness and drafts. The temperature should be around 72 degrees F. to avoid chills. Use a box with a washable blanket, and if the kitten's movement must be restricted, place a screen on top of the box with a weight on it so that the cat cannot knock the screen over.

Medicines. Liquid medicines should be given by eyedropper and poured into the side of the kitten's mouth. Pills and capsules present more of a problem. First, place the animal on a table or other surface that is level with you. Grasp the kitten's head in one hand, with your thumb and fingers pressing from opposite sides of the upper jaw. Pull the head gently backward until the nose is pointing straight up. With your other hand, pull down the lower jaw to prevent the mouth from closing. Then drop the pill or capsule on the back of the kitten's tongue, and give it a straight push with your finger so that it will go down the throat.

Never give your cat aspirin unless it is prescribed by a veterinarian. Aspirin can be very harmful to the cat's stomach.

Food. If your kitten loses its appetite, tempt it with its favorite foods. Kidney,

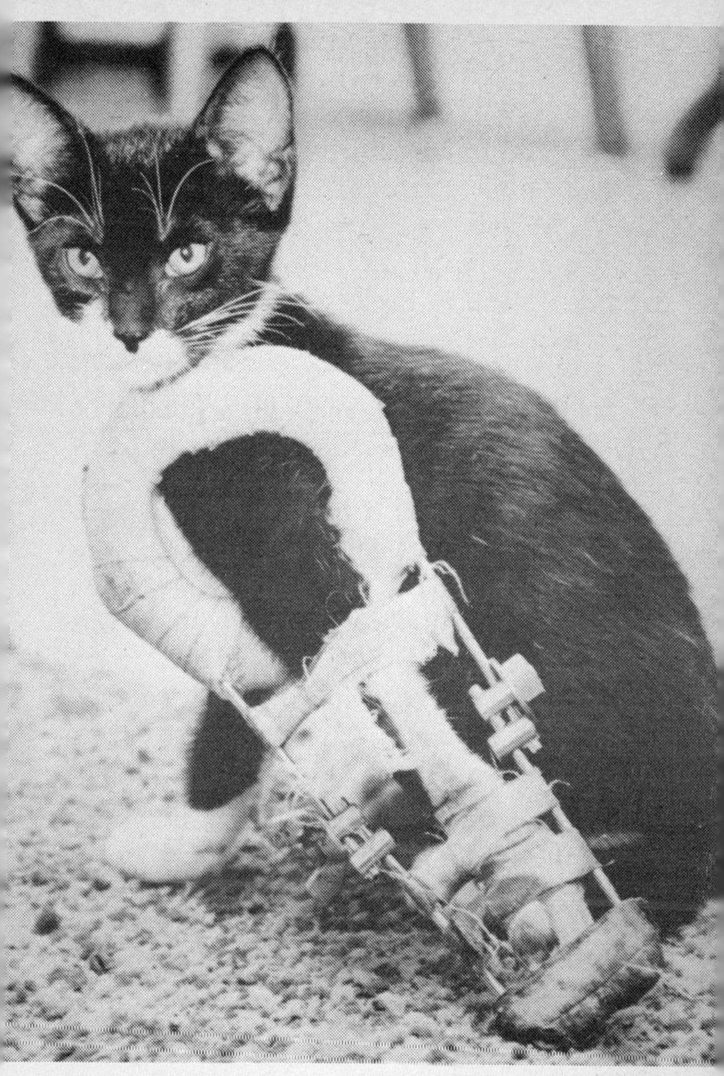

It really isn't as bad as it looks. Eight-weeks-old Duchess fell from a tree and broke her left front leg, so the leg had to be put in traction for a while. But Duchess still managed to get around.

liver, and baby food meats are good prospects. If your kitten vomits, feed it only small amounts at a time.

FIRST AID

In case your kitten meets with an accident or other catastrophe, here is what to do:

Accidents. First, protect yourself by wrapping the animal in a heavy blanket. Fright could cause it to strike out at you. If there is a heavy flow of blood, apply a bandage and hold it firmly against the wound to control bleeding until you can get to the vet.

Cuts. Let the kitten clean itself, since its tongue can do an expert cleaning job. Then, take the kitten to the veterinarian to find out if the cut should be closed with stitches. If your kitten cannot clean the cut, you can do it with hydrogen peroxide.

Bites. An immediate visit to the vet is advisable before the bite or bites have a chance to become infected.

Broken Bones. A splint should be put on the kitten even before it is taken to the vet. Since most broken bones are in the legs, a firm piece of wood or other sturdy material tied above and below the break will help keep the leg immobilized until it can be treated.

Poisoning. If your kitten has eaten poisonous material, such as paint, or chemical plant or insect sprays, feed it a mixture of one-half hydrogen peroxide and one-half water at a ratio of one teaspoon for every three pounds of weight of the kitten. Next, a very fast trip to the veterinarian.

Training Your Kitten

The only way your new kitten will know what it is and is not supposed to do, and what is expected of it, is to teach it. The sooner this training begins, the better.

Keep one fact uppermost in your mind. Like a cat, it is also impossible to force a kitten to do anything. But it is possible to encourage or discourage its actions. If you remember this, the training period will be easy and even enjoyable. Also, it may surprise you to know that a kitten is easier to train than a puppy.

BASIC EQUIPMENT

Start with the basic equipment: a cat box, a scratching board, and a bed.

Toilet Training. Cats are instinctively sanitary about their toilet habits. If you have a tray filled with sand in an appropriate place, it won't take much coaxing for your kitten to use it. All cats—from lions to domestic kittens—dig holes and cover their droppings afterward. All you should have to do is take your kitten to the tray of sand or cat litter, pick up one of its paws, and make a scratching motion. At first, there may be an occasional accident in the wrong place, but after that there should be no problem. The litter pan should be made of tin, galvanized iron, coated plastic or enamel. A flat baking tin, twelve by eighteen inches, is ideal. Metal is preferable to wood or cardboard because it does not absorb odor.

Scratching Posts. Claws are a cat's first defense. They must be sharpened constantly to stay in condition. If the outer shells of the claws are not peeled off by scratching, they grow over the claws. Scratching also keeps the muscles and tendons, which control the function of the claws, in good condition. If no scratching area is provided, the kitten will choose a sofa or your favorite easy chair. Some cats will settle for a simple log with rough bark, but most prefer a heavy board upholstered with a piece of thick carpet. A post eighteen to twenty-four inches tall is a good size, so that the kitten can stretch full-

Scratching posts need not be as elaborate as this one, which also serves as a toy and hiding place.

length when scratching. I would advise setting up your scratching post immediately, so that your kitten doesn't form the furniture habit first. If your furniture is more important than your cat and you are unwilling to take the time to train it to use the scratching post, you should think seriously before becoming a cat owner.

Some people regularly clip their cat's claws in the hope that this will prevent the animal from scratching the furniture. This really is the cat's job and should be done on its scratching post or, better still, on a tree trunk if the cat is lucky enough to have access to the outdoors. Other people go still further and remove their cat's claws. However, without its claws, a cat is completely defenseless if attacked by another animal. It cannot protect itself or escape up the bark of a tree or to some other high, safe place. Another point to consider: a cat uses its claws to express happiness. When a cat is truly contented it will "knead," or claw, the surface of whatever it is lying or sitting on. This could be you—but don't worry, it is always done gently with no intent to hurt.

Beds. You can find some very fancy cat beds in department stores and pet shops,

Cats generally decide for themselves where they will sleep. These two seem to be enjoying this basket.

but all a kitten really wants is a warm, comfortable spot. Any small basket or wooden box with a clean pillow or blanket will do. What is most important is that it is snug and out of drafts. But don't expect your kitten to settle for only one bed. It will probably find several sleeping areas in its new home.

Other Equipment. A comb and brush are necessary. A metal comb and a bristle brush made especially for a kitten's tender skin should be used every day on your pet. Toys are essential for the kitten, too, and often the simplest ones are favored. A crumpled piece of paper tied to a string, a Ping-Pong ball, or an empty paper bag can entertain a kitten as well as most commercial toys. My cats have always liked toy mice—especially the ones that squeak and are filled with catnip. I must add that their sharp claws result in a very short lifetime for the toy mouse! The best toy for a kitten, of course, is another kitten.

DISCIPLINE

All kittens learn easily and respect routine, usually one of their own making. But all kittens are stubborn. Your best bet is to *invite* them to do things. Sometimes they will do them immediately; usually only after some consideration. Be patient. As your kitten gets to know and understand you, its responses to you will be quicker and more positive.

The first thing to discourage is rough play. A well-mannered cat retracts its claws when it plays with humans. But, since this is not a natural thing for a kitten to do, you must teach your pet that there are times when it must not use its claws. Be firm, but gentle. Harshness won't help, and striking a kitten is worse than useless. Pick up the kitten's paw gently, tap the pads of its foot with one finger, and say firmly, "No." Do this every time its claws come out when it plays with you.

The situation is completely different when your kitten plays with your fingers and pretends to bite them. Then it is really playing a game and showing its affection. A cat's claws are its weapons of attack, not its teeth. Keep your hand steady. Do not move it roughly or tease the kitten. If you do, prepare for its claws to come out— with good reason!

It is almost useless to try to prevent a

kitten from jumping up on couches, chairs, and beds. And, after all, if you succeed in preventing it from scratching the furniture, what real harm can it do by curling up on a chair or bed? There are places, however, such as the dining room table or the kitchen counter, that should be forbidden territory. Shouting at the kitten or slapping a surface near it with a rolled newspaper will only scare the animal and won't really do any good. Follow the same procedure used with the claw discipline. Pick up the kitten, tap its paws gently, say "No" firmly, and place it on the floor. When you see the cat on forbidden territory or in the act of jumping up on it, repeat the process. I can almost guarantee results with this method, but I won't guarantee anything when you are not around to catch the kitten in the act!

Never pick your kitten up by the scruff of the neck as its mother does. That is the only way the mother cat can carry its young—but you have hands. Pick up the kitten by placing your hand under its body. To control an excited or frightened kitten, place one hand under the kitten's chest and hold its forelegs between your fingers. Put your other hand under its buttocks to support its body.

A kitten of eight weeks and older requires five to six meals a day; this amount should continue until it is three months old. A kitten should be fed small amounts of food often, because during this period its stomach is only about the size of a walnut.

A kitten should have at least two to three meat meals a day. When you portion out the kitten's food, keep that walnut size in mind to avoid bouts with indigestion. Space the meals so that there is time for one to be digested before the next one comes along. If possible, serve meals at the same time every day. Don't fall into the habit of giving your kitten the food it *thinks* it likes best. How many people do you know who say their cats will eat *only* this or *only* that? *These* owners have spoiled or over-fed their cats during their kittenhood. Remember a normal, active kitten never looks fat.

DIET—EIGHT WEEKS
TO TWELVE WEEKS

Breakfast   Two tablespoons of milk and egg. Beat raw yolk of one egg into contents of one-half-pint can of unsweetened evaporated milk. Amounts to twelve tablespoons if stored in refrigerator.

Mid-morning   One tablespoon raw lean meat, preferably beef, finely chopped (for variety give kidney, liver, lamb, veal, chicken); or one tablespoon canned cat food.

Luncheon   Two tablespoons milk and egg.

Mid-afternoon   One tablespoon raw, lean meat, minced; or canned cat food.

Dinner   Two tablespoons milk and egg.

Bedtime   One tablespoon raw, lean meat, minced; or canned cat food.

These three kittens were somewhat surprised to
end up sharing dinner with a baby rabbit.

If for some reason your kitten refuses to eat some or all of the food you have given it, do not leave the food in the dish. Take it away and serve fresh food for the next meal.

Some cat authorities recommend supplementing the kitten's diet with cod liver oil, brewer's yeast, or other food nutrients. However, most canned cat foods now include a good balance of nutrients, vitamins, and minerals with the meat or meat byproducts in the cans, which, in some cases, also contain milk, eggs, and vegetables.

There are many dried cat foods on the market that can be included for variety in your cat's diet. In addition to the convenience of not spoiling easily or drying up, they also help to keep your cat's teeth clean and its gums healthy.

After three months, reduce the number of meals to four while increasing their size. Try adding a little vegetable, usually about a teaspoonful of chopped green vegetables or grated carrot.

At four months, cut out one meal, reducing it to three times a day. By this time your menu should be something like this:

Breakfast	Four tablespoons milk.
Luncheon	Three tablespoons of raw meat or canned cat food, and a little vegetable.
Dinner	Three tablespoons raw meat or canned cat food; no vegetable.

After five months, meals should be cut to two a day. Always keep a supply of fresh, clean water on hand for your kitten.

At some time between six and seven months, the kitten's milk teeth are replaced by the permanent teeth. Your kitten has become a cat. It must be fed like a cat: usually one meal a day and milk, if it agrees with it. (Remember, milk is a food and does not take the place of water.) Many cat experts think that milk should be given the adult cat sparingly and some say not at all. It is an individual matter and depends on the particular cat.

A final thing to remember is the importance of raw meat in your kitten's diet. In the wild, the carnivorous cat would devour the carcass of its prey, including skin, internal organs, and bones. Although we have said that most canned cat foods are

well-balanced nutritionally, it is still advisable to include liberal amounts of raw meat
in your kitten's, and later in your cat's,
diet.

Breeds
of Cats

There are several breeds of cats recognized in the United States. These breeds have evolved naturally through the centuries or by intentional breeding. But only in recent years have cat clubs and cat shows been formed to register breeds and set up standards and specifications for them.

Several associations exist for registering cats. The oldest and largest is The Cat Fanciers Association, Inc. (It registers about 10,000 cats every year.) The American Cat Association receives most of its support in the Midwest and West, and the Cat Fanciers' Federation, Inc. is strongest in the East.

Breeds of cats can be divided into two broad categories: (1) the common housecat, a blend of many breeds and the product of chance mating; and (2) the purebred, intentionally bred to produce certain desirable characteristics. Purebreds include the pet cat and the show cat, which is trained for public showing and used mainly as breeding stock.

Cat associations issue exact specifications for accurate judging of the various breeds, and owners breed their cats to measure up to these specifications. Those that most closely meet the standards are "top quality" purebreds and bring top prices. Purebreds that do not meet the standards as well as the others bring lower prices, but are registered and make excellent house pets.

There are some 1,000 cat shows held every year in the United States, and of these about 250 are licensed cat shows. Champions and Grand Champions are selected at the licensed shows, and the cat judged best of all becomes Cat of the Year. This title is awarded by *Cats Magazine,* which keeps a record of the shows. The Cat of the Year is the winner over some 10,000 cats shown throughout the year.

Cat shows are more flexible than dog shows, at which only whole purebreds may compete. While only the whole purebred cat can win the title of Champion, there are other titles for neutered cats, purebred cats, and honors for "common" cats in what is called the Household Pet division.

Domestic shorthairs come in a variety of colors and markings.

There is no age limit for owners, but kittens must be at least four months old to qualify. If your kitten or cat is healthy, clean, well-groomed, and friendly enough to be handled by show judges, it will be welcome.

Following are the breeds recognized as eligible for showing:

DOMESTIC SHORTHAIRS

Often mistakenly called alley cats, this breed has distinct characteristics and specifications, and many are registered and exhibited at shows. They come in a variety of colors, including all white, all black, and solid patches of both. Tabbies are striped or marbled with reddish or bluish tints. The tortoise shell has patches of black, orange, and cream, and is almost always female. The calico looks like the tortoise shell except that the calico's coat contains an additional color—white. The calico's color also is sex-linked and appears almost exclusively in females. Males of both breeds are invariably sterile. If a domestic shorthair is all white, its eyes are usually blue or copper colored, and sometimes it may have one blue and one copper eye. A completely black cat is rare. Usually it has a patch of white on the chest or throat. To be considered a champion, a black cat must not have a single white hair on its coat, and it must have orange or copper eyes.

FOREIGN SHORTHAIRS

Korat. This breed has a delicate bone structure. Its body, blue-tipped with silver, is slender and its head heart-shaped. The eyes are a brilliant green-gold. The Korat's hind legs are longer than its front legs. Quiet and dignified but with a warm, affectionate nature, this breed is said to have come to the United States from Thailand.

A two-and-a-half-year-old Korat called Pyewacket.

Burmese. A sturdy, stocky body identifies this breed as do a rounded head and rounded ears. Gentler and less demanding than the Siamese, the Burmese is the result of deliberate crossings by breeders. It has a rich brown color with lighter tones of brown on its underparts. The Burmese eye color ranges from yellow to gold.

Abyssinian. More powerful than the Burmese, the "Aby" has a lithe, long body, a whiplike tail, and large, almond-shaped eyes, which are yellow, green, or hazel. This breed has "ticked" fur, or fur in which each hair is marked by two or three bands of color—silver, brown, or black.

Siamese. Most popular of the foreign shorthairs, Siamese are lean and graceful with a long head and tapered tail. Extremely sensitive, they are more curious than most cats and their insistent, high-pitched cry is hard to ignore. Body colors are cream and dark brown (Seal Point); cream and chocolate brown (Chocolate Point); white with blue shading (Blue Point); and off-white and frosted gray with pinkish tones (Lilac Point, also called Frost Point). All Siamese cats have blue eyes.

Pedro, an eighteen-month-old Burmese, has learned to open the door when he wants to go out.

The Abyssinian has a long body and a whiplike tail.

This handsome Seal Point Siamese male is Kar-
nak Zapata, Cat Fanciers' Association's Cat of
the Year in 1971.

Russian Blue. This breed has a long, graceful body and large ears. Unlike other shorthairs, its coat does not lie smooth against the body, but is short and thick and stands away from the skin. The color is bright blue and the longer hairs are silver-tipped. The eyes are a vivid green.

British Blue. Much like the Russian Blue, the British Blue has a delicate body with tipped ears. Its coat is lavender blue and its eyes are a brilliant green.

Chartreux. The coat color of the Chartreux is similar to the Russian and British Blues, but the body is like a miniature lion, with stocky shoulders and full chest. The eyes are large, round, and orange-tinted. This little-known breed comes from Europe.

Havana Brown. A cross between the Siamese and the Domestic Shorthair, this breed has large eyes and large, rounded ears. The coat is a rich mahogany brown and the eyes are light green.

Rex. This relatively new breed is distinctive for its short, curly hair, which resembles the coat of a Persian lamb. Its body is long and muscular, and its coat can be many different colors.

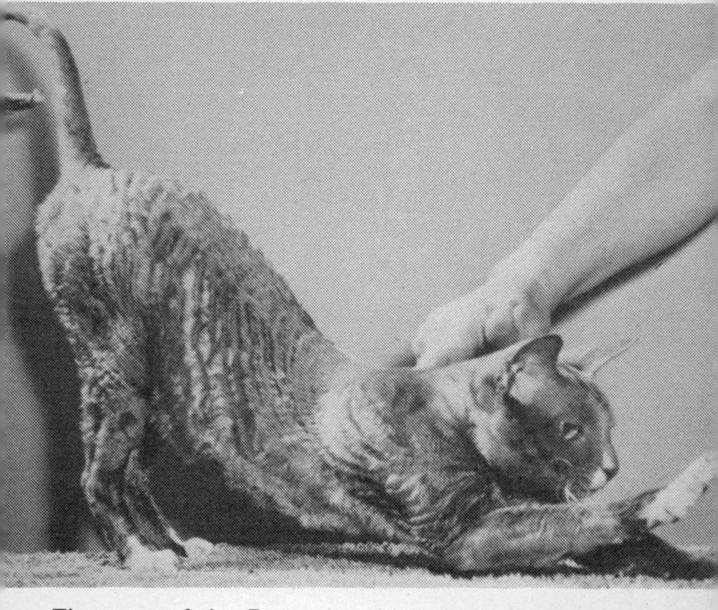

The coat of the Rex resembles that of a Persian lamb. Note that even the whiskers are curled.

The Manx is usually tailless. This is a nearly three-year-old female, known as Nike.

Manx. The Manx is usually considered the tailless cat because the show breed must have no tail. Many others, however, do have tails of varying lengths. The back legs are longer than the front legs, and the head is large and round. Its colors are many.

Harlequin. The only spotted white cat known, the "best" according to cat show judges, carries a single black spot on its head, none or up to ten on its body, and a solid black, blunt tail. The spots are about the size of nickels. The coat is thick and the body Manx-like. Harlequins are rare and bring top prices.

LONGHAIRS

Long-haired breeds are more similar in body type than shorthairs. They have "cobby" bodies—low on the legs and deep in the chest. They have large heads and round eyes, broad, stubby noses, and well-rounded ears. Their silky coats cover a sturdy, bony skeleton and strong muscles. Longhairs come in five solid colors (white, cream, black, blue, and red) and in several patterns or markings (tabbies, shaded pat-

World champion of the International Cat Show, Paris, 1950, is an eighteen-month-old white Persian with the distinguished name of Farquar Aiglon.

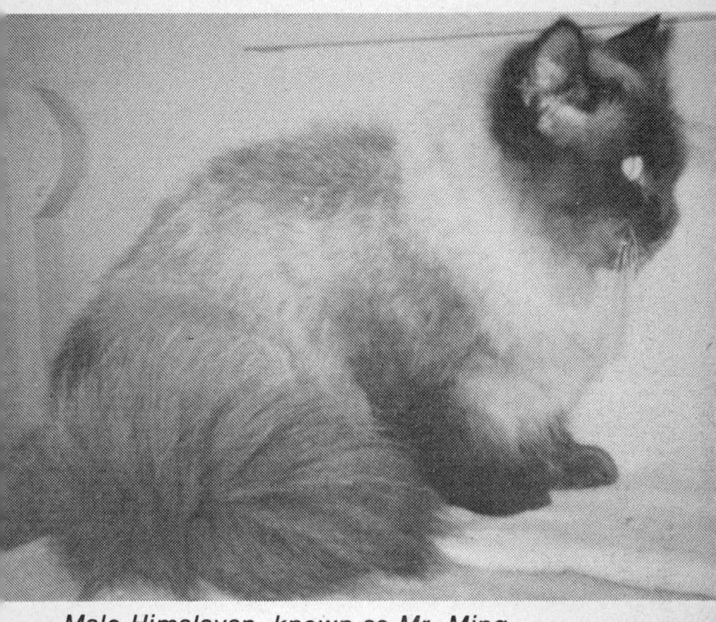

Male Himalayan, known as Mr. Ming.

terns, smokes, tipped, or ticked designs and tri-colors). Their long, luxuriant coats require constant grooming to maintain beauty and comfort.

Persians. Most popular of all longhairs, Persians, with their manes across the neck and back of the ears resemble miniature lions. Persians' eyes can be any color as long as they complement or contrast the coat, and the coat is usually divided into three color divisions. They are (solid—blue, black, red, cream, and white; (2) silver; and (3) patched or tabby—many colored.

Himalayan. Himalayans are the result of deliberate crossings of Siamese with Persians. The body type and coat is Persian-like, and the deep blue color is like the Siamese.

Birman. Sometimes called the Sacred Cat of Burma, the Birman's markings are similar to the Siamese except that the hair is long, the body heavier, and the color always golden. The Birman's feet are all pure white.

Balinese. A relatively new breed, the Balinese has all the color combinations and characteristics of the Siamese except that it is longhaired.

Female Balinese kitten

Maine Coon Cat. This breed could be called a semilonghair; it is longer than the shorthair and shorter than the longhair. Many are black and white, but they can be several different colors. The eye color corresponds to the color of the coat. The Maine Coon cat, a generally large specimen, can weigh sixteen pounds or more when grown. Many people think, incorrectly, that the breed is the result of crossing a cat with a raccoon. It did, in fact, develop from the interbreeding of cats brought back from foreign lands by Maine sailors in the 1880's.

Maine Coon kittens. To the left is a blue female called Wendy, and to the right is a red male who answers (at least when he feels like it) to the name of Bobby McGee.

Your
New Friend

Whatever kitten you select—longhair, shorthair, foreign, or domestic—of course, is up to you. I have owned purebreds and plain housecats and have been very fond of every one of them.

No matter what the breed, the important thing is to give your kitten love and affection, and also to provide it with firm discipline when necessary.

Just before I finished this book, a seven-week-old kitten came to live with me. "E.B." is a bouncing, black, domestic shorthair who put my words on feeding, care, and discipline in this book to a very real test! We have our clashes, E.B. and I, but we have become the best of friends, and I find him to be a delightful, affectionate, and loving companion who knows his own mind.

Paul Gallico, who has written much about cats as well as other subjects, sums up the charming independence of the cat in this selection from his book *The Abandoned:*

When in Doubt—Wash

If you have committed any kind of an error and anyone scolds you—wash. If you slip and fall off something and somebody laughs at you—wash.

If somebody calls you and you don't care to come and still you don't wish to make it a direct insult—wash. Something hurt you? Wash it.

Door closed and you're burning up because no one will open it for you—have yourself a little wash and forget it. Somebody petting another cat or dog in the same room, and you are annoyed over that—be nonchalant; wash. Feel sad—wash away your blues.

And—of course you also wash to get clean and to keep clean.

The American Cat Association
16318 Lakewood Boulevard
Bellflower, California 90706
(and)
P.O. Box 3637
Austin, Texas 78704

The Cat Fanciers Association, Inc
P.O. Box 430
Red Bank, New Jersey 07701

Cat Fanciers' Federation, Inc.
3485 Linwood Road
Cincinnati, Ohio 45226

Crown Cat Fanciers Association
Route 3, Box 347½
Huntsville, Alabama 35806

Independent Cat Federation
275 Washington Street
Cambridge, Massachusetts 02140

National Cat Fanciers'
Association
6812 Gahona Avenue
Allen Park, Michigan 48101

The United Cat Federation, Inc.
6616 East Hereford Drive
Los Angeles, California 90022

Cat
Publications

Two of the best publications devoted to cats, which can be found in most libraries, are:

Cats Magazine
10 California Avenue
Pittsburgh, Pennsylvania 15202

Published monthly with news, pictures, tips, calendars of show dates and places, and listings of leading breeders.

Cat Fancy
11760 Sorrento Valley Road
San Diego, California 92121

Published bimonthly with informative articles, short fiction, and full-color art.

Index

ABOUT THE AUTHOR

JANE ROCKWELL has been an animal lover since her childhood and has owned a number of cats. She was born in St. Paul, Minnesota, and attended the University of Nebraska. She has done graduate work in art and writing at the University of Chicago, New York University, and the New School for Social Research.

Ms. Rockwell enjoys gardening and sailing. She lives in Ridgefield, Connecticut, where she works as a free-lance writer and editor. *Cats and Kittens* is her first book for young people. She is also the author of *Dogs and Puppies,* now available in an Archway Paperback edition.

Ms. Doll of Miami

Breadcrumbs Lisi

Blossom

E.B.

Rachel of Hartsdale

Cassandra and Family

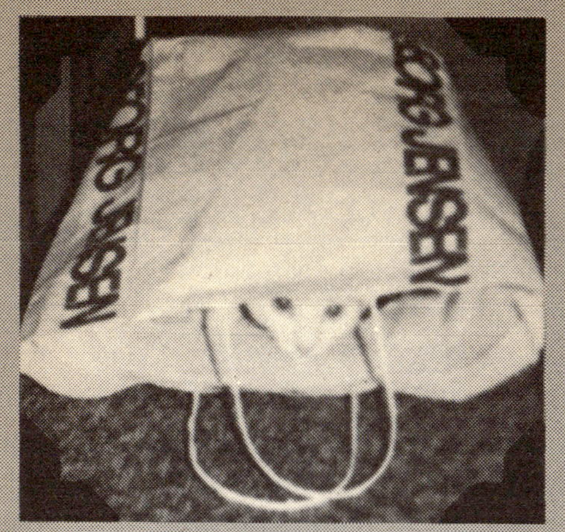

Mr. Benchley

Hecate

29895 MISS OSBORNE-THE-MOP, by Wilson Gage. Illustrated by Paul Galdone. Jody has a wacky and wonderful summer when she discovers that she has acquired unexpected magical powers. ($1.50)

56036 JUST A DOG, by Helen Griffiths. Illustrated by Victor Ambrus. An abandoned mongrel pup roams the streets of a large city, facing hunger and fear. After many adventures, she finally finds the home and security she seeks. ($1.75)

29983 DANNY DUNN AND THE SMALLIFYING MACHINE, by Jay Williams and Raymond Abrashkin. Illustrated by Paul Sagsoorian. When Danny gets trapped in Professor Bullfinch's latest invention, he shrinks to insect size and must face survival in a world that has become a giant jungle. ($1.50)

29726 THE HAPPY DOLPHINS, by Samuel Carter III. Illustrated with photographs. The author explores many intriguing facets of dolphin behavior as he tells the true story of Dal and Suwa, two bottle-nosed dolphins that made friends with humans. ($1.25)

56083 MISHMASH, by Molly Conc. Illustrated by Leonard Shortall. Life is full of surprises for Pete when he gets Mishmash—a huge, black, friendly hound who turns the whole town topsy-turvy with his hilarious doings. ($1.50)

29787 TALL AND PROUD, by Vian Smith. Illustrated by Don Stivers. Her very own horse—an impossible dream come true—inspires Gail to overcome the fear and pain of polio and learn to walk and ride again. ($1.25)

29816 MOSHIE CAT, by Helen Griffiths. Illustrated by Shirley Hughes. The true story of a Majorcan kitten's adventures and misadventures as he searches for and finds a loving home. ($1.25)

29778 THE HOUSE OF THIRTY CATS, by Mary Calhoun. Illustrated by Mary Chalmers. Adventure and excitement enter Sarah's life when she pays her first visit to Miss Tabitha's wonderful house, meets the members of the cat community, and chooses a kitten of her very own. ($1.50)

29866 BASIL AND THE PYGMY CATS, by Eve Titus. Illustrated by Paul Galdone. Follow Basil to the mysterious East in one of the most perplexing cases of his famed career as the Sherlock Holmes of the mouse community. ($1.25)

29996 "NATIONAL VELVET," by Enid Bagnold. When Velvet Brown won a piebald in a village raffle, she began a glorious adventure that would take her all the way to the Grand National, the greatest race in the world. ($1.75)